D1623992

THE LIBRARY OF CONTEMPORARY THOUGHT

*America's most original voices
tackle today's most provocative issues*

HARRY SHEARER

IT'S THE STUPIDITY, STUPID
*Why (Some) People Hate Clinton
and Why the Rest of Us Have to Watch*

"We are told by nostalgic conservatives (shouldn't nostalgia be the official emotion of conservatives?) that Ronald Reagan so respected the Oval Office that he never took his jacket off while he was within its confines. For some reason, that image seems to persist in their memories far better than the trading of arms for hostages. . . .

"As in so many other ways, Clinton has fallen short. Reagan was America's best supporting man, the leading man's best friend; Clinton has become America's stand-in, his cheeseball draft evasion substituting for the draft-card-burning lovers of Ho Chi Minh, his non-inhaling experiment on foreign shores standing in for empty-eyed acidheads begging for spare change on our street corners, his furtive fumbling for hallway blow jobs standing in for John and Yoko naked in bed on the world's TV screens."

IT'S THE STUPIDITY, STUPID

Why (Some) People Hate
Clinton and Why the Rest
of Us Have to Watch

HARRY SHEARER

THE LIBRARY OF CONTEMPORARY THOUGHT
THE BALLANTINE PUBLISHING GROUP • NEW YORK

The Library of Contemporary Thought
Published by The Ballantine Publishing Group

Copyright © 1999 by Harry Shearer

http://www.randomhouse.com/BB/

Library of Congress Cataloging-in-Publication Data
Shearer, Harry.
It's the stupidity, stupid : why (some) people hate Clinton and why
the rest of us have to watch / Harry Shearer.—1st ed.
p.   cm.
ISBN 0-345-43401-3 (hc. : alk. paper)
1. Clinton, Bill, 1946– —Public opinion. 2. Clinton, Bill, 1946–
—Sexual behavior. 3. Clinton, Bill, 1946– —Humor. 4. Public
opinion—United States—History—20th century. 5. United
States—Politics and government—1993- 6. Political corruption—
United States—Public opinion—History—20th century. I. Title.
E886.2.S43   1999
973.929' 092—dc21   98-51294
                                                 CIP

Text design by Holly Johnson
Cover design by Ruth Ross
Cover illustration by Carlos Torres

Manufactured in the United States of America

First Edition: February 1999

10   9   8   7   6   5   4   3   2   1

To my mom and to Judith

Acknowledgments

Peter Gethers solicited my involvement in this series of little books, and he is totally, personally, 100 percent responsible for the opinions expressed herein. Sue him. His encouragement and support contrast nicely with the behavior of show-business people, so the entire publishing industry has not yet succumbed. Carol Ross Joynt and Arianna Huffington, two of my best and most contrasting friends, stimulated some of the thinking found herein, assuming there is any, and they too bear full responsibility for the contents. Sue them also. Ruth Seymour at KCRW, public radio in Santa Monica, has allowed me to do political comedy on *Le Show* for fifteen years now, so she is uniquely to blame for what I've written here. Don't sue her; it will only increase the length of the next fund drive. I'd like to thank CNN, CNBC, Fox News Channel, and particularly MSNBC for making this whole story so ubiquitous that O.J. Simpson's return to the news late last year seemed like a breath of fresh air. They also made the Clinton-Lewinsky saga so well known that less exposition was necessary, and I could cut straight to the chase. That makes them responsible for the chase. Please sue them. Finally, I'd like to thank the voters and politicians of America for making this book both possible and necessary. You know who you are. Sue yourselves.

Contents

CONTENTS

Introduction: What's the Question?

IN THE AFTERMATH OF, shall we say, certain events, it seems almost cretinous to ask why some people hate the forty-second president of the United States. Bill Clinton let down his friends and followers and subordinates, caused no end of legal fees to many of them, and, more ominously, made it possible for William Bennett to unleash upon the public yet another bilious stream of self-righteous posturings. Bennett, whose advocacy of mandatory minimum prison sentences for nonviolent drug offenders necessitated a cell-clearing release of thousands of murderers and rapists, remains the most dangerous man in America, a neo-Puritan gasbag who'd organize witch burnings if he didn't fear that proximity to flame might tempt him to resume his longtime cigarette habit.

Clinton, smart enough to be a *Jeopardy* champion, couldn't figure out that the rules governing public figures had changed since the heyday of JFK and his molls, and through his recklessness (and the insatiably prurient curiosity of his detractors, of which he was ever aware) he introduced a generation of subteens to the ideas of fellatio and sex toys years before their mothers were prepared to tell them to ask their fathers. He and his supporters helped make sexual harassment a highly profitable new area of legal practice, and then he chose as his sex partner the least powerful, least credentialed woman cleared into his official compound. And certainly Clinton, who derived great popularity from crusading for years against the tobacco industry, should have anticipated the negative publicity attendant on using a cigar as an erotic implement.

His recent stupidity has been appalling, almost as much so as the stupidity he exhibited in the halcyon days of health-care reform. Back then, you may recall, he sent the missus out for a well-regarded week of congressional testimony, then retired from the field of public contention while the insurance industry blanketed the airwaves with commercials featuring the frightened and frightening Harry and

Louise. The president behaved as if in the big leagues the opposition wilts once the votes have been counted, as if the cozy one-party politics of Little Rock had moved up to D.C. along with the Clintons and the Tyson chicken gang. "Smart people acting stupid" may well be the epitaph of this administration. Hillary Rodham, after all, helped draft the rules for considering the last presidential impeachment.

The most-hated presidents of this century up to now have been Franklin Roosevelt and Richard Nixon. FDR, whose marriage may yet turn out to be the template for the Clintons' (he and Eleanor both had girlfriends), ran on a platform of balancing the budget to cure the Depression, then did a one-eighty once in office, importing fifty-year-old European reforms such as Social Security and unemployment insurance in a desperate attempt to keep the economy from flatlining until a war could apply the paddles to its ticker. Nixon, who lacked the social skills to be an undertaker, left a landscape of savaged careers under his personal career ladder. After a quarter century of calling anyone unfortunate enough to get in his way a Communist, a pinko, a fellow traveler, or part of the conspiracy to "lose" China to the "Reds," he became a foreign-policy sage by recognizing that China was, in fact, run by the Communists, and made the world safe for his secretary of state Henry Kissinger to become the Reds' chief lobbyist. Both men stood for something, even if it was something diametrically opposed to the ideologies upon which they built their careers.

Truman, until his recent elevation to the Mt. Rushmore waiting room, was reviled as a hick not worthy to shine Roosevelt's wheels. Eisenhower, whose geniality was widely believed to exceed his intelligence, was the laughingstock of smarties who delighted in the incoherence of his press-conference ramblings. Kennedy let Martin Luther King Jr. and Earl Warren take the brunt of the ambient hatred that suffused his era. Lyndon Johnson was despised for backing his way into a war that, as it turns out, neither he nor his defense secretary believed in. Only later did we learn that the "hallowed Oval Office," now being cited as the victim of Clintonian degradation, was the place where LBJ invited hapless Cabinet members to join him in a trip to the bathroom, where they had to watch him defecate while policy options got thrashed out.

Gerald Ford won scorn for pardoning Nixon, and pity for being shot at. Only as a money-grubbing ex-president has he qualified for true obloquy, but nobody notices.

Reagan infuriated his opponents in a way that has recent echoes. The more he was revealed to be a genial napper whose meetings with other officials were dominated by his show-business anecdotes, the more the public liked him. I was at a dinner party late in Reagan's second term with a network White House correspondent who regaled the table with the most recent evidence that the president had what the Tower Commission memorably described as a "hands-off management style." After about fifteen minutes of this, a liberal comedian at the table exploded beyond the bounds of genial banter. "How come," he demanded of the journalist, "you don't put this stuff on TV?" The correspondent looked at the comedian as if he were nuts. "Because," he intoned in his best network voice, "we read the polls. The public doesn't want to hear it." Subordinates, like Reagan's attorney general ("Experts Agree, Meese Is a Pig" proclaimed a T-shirt) and his interior secretary (who seemed to believe the only species worth preserving was *Christianus bornagainus*), attracted all the venom.

Bush carried the suspicions of the CIA-distrusters into office with him, and earned the contempt of tax-cutting Republicans when his thin parson's lips betrayed him.

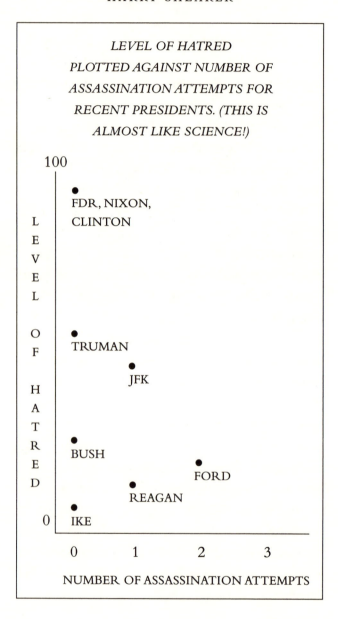

But, aside from FDR and Nixon, none of the presidents within living memory inspired dogged, persistent, indefatigable movements to get their asses out of the White House. Bill Clinton, somehow, managed to join this select company.

Yet much of the contempt for Clinton, outside the coterie of the true haters, has been rooted in his pathos. Why didn't he pick great-looking, accomplished women for his conquests? Jack Kennedy proved, after all, that the presidency opens up the world's largest à la carte menu of willing socialites and movie stars. And if Clinton wanted to have sex with some google-eyed intern, why didn't he just bang her, instead of insisting on the double diddling that will serve as the metaphor of his term in office?

None of this answers the question of why William Jefferson Clinton accumulated a crowd of rabid haters around him from the moment he moved into a White House they were sure he had usurped. Neither will the rest of what you'll read here. Hey, it's an imperfect world.

But the journey we're about to go on (I'm borrowing a Clintonian word here; having your pathetically adolescent sex life humiliatingly revealed to a bored public is a "journey") could be a useful one—especially for me if you've paid for this book and aren't just browsing through it at the airport. Some Republicans have been aching to avenge the demise of the Nixon presidency for a quarter century, but not until Clinton's ascendance could they count on a dependable reservoir of truly motivated hating talent. If a small cadre of haters can target a president, knowing his personality flaws, and entrap him into the kind of behavior that any sane person would cover up, it would be important to know what motivated them—if for no other reason than to help us prepare to grease the skids under the next guy.

1

Three-fourths of *Hate* Is *Hat*

THIS LITTLE BOOK IS about hatred. Hatred has a bad name these days, primarily because the notion has been spread around that hating folks is reason enough to take violent action against them. That notion we can call, in verbal shorthand, the history of the twentieth century.

But hatred can and should be its own reward, savored for its ability to fuel baroque revenge fantasies that can be replayed for at least as much personal enjoyment as bizarre sex scenarios. My wife is of the belief, widely shared, that hating someone or some carefully selected group (such as, let's pick at random, expatriate Canadian comedy producers) is bad for one's health, stoking the body to produce—I don't know, her theory gets a little vague here, but I guess the pseudoscientific thrust of it would be something like bad vibes lead to increased oxidation, which leads to . . . whatever it is that antioxidants are supposed to prevent.

If that theory were true, the converse might also be true, and we baby boomers, who marinated ourselves in infinite varieties of love in our incredibly prolonged youth, should be the healthiest people in human history. Maybe we are, but we still seem to be dropping off at a rate that seems pretty normal, although the Gen Xers behind us must find it agonizingly slow.

So I'm not anti-hatred. In its proper place, like hot pepper, it helps make life worth living. When the guy in the Toyota Corolla two lanes away decides that he has, absolutely *has,* to make a left turn, and the only way to do that is to veer directly across your path without benefit of so much as a "Hey, do you mind?" you could spend your day loving him. But since when do they have traffic near ashrams? Over the years I've made it a practice to imagine large, goiter-like growths on the necks of people who've made parts of my existence a living hell, and except for the fact that the growths never materialize, I've found it an entirely satisfying experience.

On the other hand, just as peppering a cantaloupe would be wrong, directing hatred at an object not really hateworthy is a waste of a precious internal resource. After all, only the very few of us who live in cabins in Montana or do daily talk radio have an infinite supply of hate. And the reason I'm writing and you're reading (we could reverse the relationship after we get to know each other a little better; we'll see) is to figure out why, of all people, Bill Clinton has inspired such profound and persistent hatred in a sufficient number of Americans to propel his presidency to the "kinda like Nixon" section of the history books.

We are, after all, talking about a man whose two heroes were a rock singer who wrote almost none of his songs and a president who was killed before accomplishing anything except taking us to the brink of nuclear war. Having thus chosen his role models, he dodged the draft with no more nor less grace than most of us (I personally refused induction, but that's another book—*100 Greatest Draft Stories,* a coffee-table book of the baby boom's coming of age, not sold in stores), and sampled pot with fewer inhales than most of us (at the time, inhaling seemed to be a critical part of the sampling process; doing without it is tantamount to gargling without liquid). This is severely middling stuff.

And, of course, the middling didn't stop there. Bill Clinton's instincts for the absolute center of everything have been so profound through the years that, had the politics thing not worked out, he could have hired on with any highway department in the country to paint the double yellow lines freehand. It's a skill that has served him well. After all, before Clinton, the Democratic (or, as the Republicans like to call it, the Democrat) Party had allowed itself to be thoroughly identified with the (here's a late-eighties usage for you) *l*-word, meaning that there were then still some ways in which Democrats could be distinguished from Republicans.

Clinton argued, successfully, that such distinctions worked against the Democrats' electoral success, and before you knew it, foreign banks and homegrown tobacco companies were finding the donkey's coffers almost as welcome a depository for their excess funds as the elephant's. While campaigning strenuously for campaign finance reform, Clinton equally strenuously continued to play by the old rules. This could have earned him the dismay of the Common Cause gang, but they're so evolved that they merely hate the system, not the people who keep it going.

Once installed, Clinton made his mark almost immediately by sequentially finding himself on opposing sides of the same issues: Gays should (shouldn't) serve in the military, nannies should (shouldn't) be screwed out of their Social Security benefits, health care should (shouldn't) be taken over by managed-competition alliances. (On that latter point, incidentally, I should just point out that anybody in show business could tell you that it's a bad idea to have anything taken over by an outfit whose initials are MCA.) Among the friends and foes he began to accumulate, there wasn't one good screech-out-your-lungs hater among them. Lani Guinier can probably restrain her admiration for Clinton, but the evidence suggests that she, in our current usage, has gone on with the rest of her life. The insurance companies that steamrollered Hillarycare, and which more recently helped kill the HMO reform bill, are probably happier today than they were before we knew who Ira Magaziner is (assuming that it's possible to really know who Ira Magaziner is).

Welfare advocates despise the bill that Clinton signed, which reformed welfare the way Terminix reforms termites, but they acknowledge with a sigh that he did so only after the Republicans won the Congress and were determined to go even farther. Civil-liberties proponents still grumble quietly about retreats on habeas corpus and immigrants' rights that Clinton acceded to, but they defend to the death his right to do so.

On policy grounds, the man has been mushier than the output of the Gerber factory. Basically, he's been an amiable gent of considerable intelligence who's presided over a whacking great economy without getting us into too much trouble overseas. In other words, he wanted to be Kennedy, and he ended up being Eisenhower. There's your karma, and your irony to boot. Not much to admire, but what's to hate?

Clearly, the question has been vexing to those in the White House as well. Hillary Clinton has taken two shots at an answer, both of them goofy enough to suggest that she never again be allowed to operate heavy machinery.

Her first attempt, of course, was "the vast right-wing conspiracy," a suggestion launched on the *Today* show, where ideas vie with centenarians' birthday salutes and viewers' egg boiling for brevity. "Vast conspiracy" hasn't yet made it onto the ubiquitously e-mailed list of the top fifty oxymorons, but it should be bubbling under. A conspiracy by its nature should be a fairly tightly controlled operation, like the Mafia or Scientology. Vastness is okay for blandly disturbing phenomena like Madonna or Seinfeld, but it has no place in the realm of conspiratorial projects. If you wanted to sabotage a presidency and you were as rich as Richard Mellon Scaife, you might want to limit word of this project to a few hundred of your closest friends and most slavish followers.

Also, there are plenty of conservatives—well, not plenty, but some—who didn't clock in regularly as part of Ken Starr's media strike force. Of the gang of "revolutionaries" installed in the House leadership after the 1994 election, only Tom DeLay has staked out a rabidly anti-Clinton position, and that may merely be a vestige of his former career as an exterminator. Dick Armey has been virtually silent on the subject of Clinton, and what good is a silent Dick Armey? Even Newt Gingrich, the original string puller behind the House impeachment machine, has vacillated in his public statements. He once threatened to insert a mention of Clinton's "crimes" (*scandals,* he told Christian conservatives, wasn't a sufficiently venomous word to describe what was going on in the White House) into every statement he made. He then proceeded to drop the subject like a cancer-ridden first wife. Ultimately, of course, the former Speaker enjoyed a singular distinction: although Monica Lewinsky gave Bill Clinton oral sex, it was Newt Gingrich she ended up screwing.

Hillary's second attempt at explaining the splenetic attacks on Clinton was even more peculiar. The fury directed at her husband and her, she told an Arkansas newspaper, could be attributed to anti-Arkansas sentiment. Well, I defer to no one in the depth of my anti-Arkansas sentiment. Arkansas is like Alabama, but with fewer teeth. Arkansans raise so many chickens because it's the only animal they're smarter than. Arkansas is what happens when Texans marry their cousins.

That being said, it should be noted that Hillary Clinton was raised in Illinois and educated at Wellesley. She's as identified with Arkansas as the cast of *Forbidden Broadway*. Coming from Arkansas didn't get one of Bill Clinton's mentors, the late Senator Fulbright, hated, even though it did force him to adopt the nuttiest political course imaginable: He was the world's only segregationist opponent of the Vietnam War. Back in the days, Georgia held as many lynchings as Arkansas, yet there was no Georgiaphobic response to Jimmy Carter.

A powerful, regionally prejudiced animus

toward Bill Clinton could logically be centered only in our nation's capital, the premise being that Washington loathes him for his outsiderness and is determined to punish him for it. It's true that Americans love to send "outsiders" to the capital: Reagan, Carter, Clinton, Sonny Bono—people who have spent years campaigning against the evil District of Columbia and every part of its way of being (see Clinton's 1992 attacks on "the brain-dead politics of the past"). But the D.C. locals are pros—that's exactly why we distrust them—and they've seen this outsider act more often than hip-hop fans have seen baggy jeans and untied shoelaces. They don't hate these newcomers; they suck 'em in, teach them the secret handshake, let them in on the game. Co-opting outsiders is a more familiar part of the Washington scene than waiting for the cherry blossoms or lobbying your former colleagues.

Besides, running against Washington is always good politics precisely because nobody west of the Potomac gives a damn about what people in Washington think. The true Clinton haters wouldn't know K Street from a breakfast cereal. Arkansas is safe.

SOME THINGS AND PEOPLE IT'S STILL SAFE TO HATE

Maybe one reason some people hate Clinton so much is that it's become culturally unpopular, not to mention dangerous, to hate much else. Here's the dwindling list (it'll be shorter in the second edition) of what it's still okay to despise:

1. Airline food
2. Telemarketing
3. Canadians (not including French Canadians, who are very prickly)
4. Television
5. John Tesh
6. The guys who yell at you in the promos for TV shows
7. People with body or mouth odor stronger than your own
8. Rush Limbaugh/Howard Stern (it's the same person, he just takes off his wig at noon and puts on his fat suit)

9. Bill Gates/Rupert Murdoch (again, the same person, but one of them didn't have to buy his citizenship)
10. Neighbors who play their music too loud, especially if it's John Tesh music
11. Neighbors who complain that your music's too loud
12. Linda Tripp
13. Charts and lists inserted into small books just to pad them out, usually at the editor's insistence

2

Hatred without the *R* Is *Death*

A VERY WISE MAN once said that all hatred
stems from self-hatred. Of course, I don't remember who he is, and it's quite likely that I made
him up. But the point remains. Do the haters hate
Clinton because he reminds them of themselves?

Let's see: He's brilliant and manipulative, good-
looking and needy. They're . . . good-looking.

Actually, Larry Klayman, the chief litigator for
the Clinton haters, is a pretty smart guy. Freed
from the constraints of having to earn a living by
the contributions of viewers like you, he's been
able to cram Bill Clinton's life with more lawsuits
than fill Judge Judy's docket in a yearful of episodes.
Larry Nichols, another Clinton-hating Larry, is reported to be bitter over Clinton's role in severing

him from the world of work, and persons whose behavior stems from such an exceptional if understandable sense of grievance are usually written off by their postal supervisors as "disgruntled ex-employees." Has Nichols recruited a sizable group of followers around the cause of rehiring Larry Nichols? Not very likely.

Much of Bill Clinton's life story is admirable, the stuff of which dumb-ass schoolbooks are made. The son of an alcoholic father, he rose out of near poverty to be a Rhodes scholar. That's an impressive-sounding accomplishment, at least until you realize what the qualifications are for Rhodes scholars. They're not the smartest kids in college, nor are they the most talented. Cecil Rhodes, in setting up the scholarship program, specified that the recipients should be "well-rounded" young men. Let's be kind and assume he wasn't speaking anatomically. He wanted to reward kids who spent as much time on the football team as in the library. The brainiest of the jocks, the jockiest of the brains. Don't get me wrong—getting a Rhodes is still a much bigger deal than being the kid who poses for the suit ads in the college paper, but I'll bet you the royalties for this book that virtually none of the people at NASA were Rhodes scholars. Incidentally, "virtually none" is the kind of Clintonian weasel-wording that can keep you from ever winning that bet.

But at least we're in fertile territory for hatred here. Americans don't like smart people. Three of the least-liked persons in our country today are Clinton, Ken Starr, and Newt Gingrich, and all of them are the sort of fellow who reads the front section of the newspaper first. Being a brainy guy has always raised suspicions in this country. Men of action are more admired than men of words. Stallone makes more money than Woody Allen. Even Frank Stallone.

THE FIVE SMARTEST
AMERICANS TO BE
TRULY HATED

1. *McGeorge Bundy and Robert MacNamara (tie).* At the height of the Vietnam War, when teenagers actually knew the names of the national security adviser and the defense secretary, there was a clear

---

reason to hate those individuals—
they wanted your ass in a rice
paddy.

2. *Malcolm X.* His speeches don't
sound nearly as scary now as when
he first made them, but he had a
fiery style (and a desire not to take
orders from Elijah Muhammad)
that drove a lot of people straight
to rabid fury.

3. *Robert Bork.* His voice sounds like
it's filtered through a bathtub
drain, and he pines for a Supreme
Court that could hew to the
Founders' intent with opinions
like the Dred Scott decision. The
liberals thought they punished him
by denying him a seat on the court
in a nomination fight that
ratcheted up the standard for
nastiness, but his real punishment
has arrived lately: A man who
despises the electronic age has

become a regular guest on *Larry King Live*.

4. *Gloria Steinem.* She probably single-handedly closed the Playboy Clubs, and she was responsible for the marital-status-neutral title *Ms.*, which caught on momentarily. Conservative women hated her for being so good-looking; conservative men hated her for not shutting up.

5. *Martin Luther King Jr.* The next time somebody says Bill Clinton can't exert moral leadership because he got blow jobs in the office, bring up this name: While running a sex life so active that he kept J. Edgar Hoover riveted to the wiretap earphones, King managed to jump-start a nonviolent revolution. Talk about compartmentalizing.

Anti-intellectualism, like hatred itself, isn't all bad. After all, it was the smarties who got us into Vietnam, the best and the brightest who analogized the geopolitics of Southeast Asia to the game of dominoes. It was the people who don't snicker at the notion of political "science" who, during the 1980s, had us "tilting" back and forth between Iran and Iraq, as if, by the precise and proper calibration of the amount of arms we shipped their way, we could make either one of them be our friend. "Common sense" is the most valued commodity in American politics, as if a policy on the Asian economic crisis or NATO expansion is the sort of thing that, if you just sit on your front porch chewing straw for a half hour or so, will come to you as naturally as the right way to drain the septic tank.

So there's something about Bill Clinton the policy wonk that always rubbed us the wrong way. Who in his right mind would want to spend New Year's Eve at thought-provoking seminars with Robert Reich, for God's sake? Renaissance Weekend always sounded like something organized by people who didn't get dates for the prom, who wanted to prove that, since high school, they had developed far finer forms of enjoyment than were available to the rest of us. Me, I'll take Dick Clark, freezing his Botox off on that Times Square balcony, anytime.

3

People Who Don't Hate Clinton

PEOPLE IN HOLLYWOOD DON'T hate Bill Clinton. As a matter of fact, they continue to insist that he accept great gobs of money from them as often as legally possible. His recent travails have only increased their sympathetically lucrative response to him. And no wonder. If anyone had a hard choice to make about the president during 1998, it was Hollywood folks.

If they turned on him, denounced him for betraying their high hopes, or agonized over his lack of judgment, they would have been reviled as hypocrites. These, after all, are the people who bombard us with the vilest kind of mindless crap, then blame us for it. Pornographers give us what we want, too, but at least they have the sensitivity and good taste to work under assumed names. On the other hand, if the Hollywood folks were too public in their support of Clinton, they risked marking him as one of them, stripping him of his last vestige of just-folksness. When a guy's last remaining friends are people whose only hierarchical distinctions are between millionaires and billionaires, it's not even remotely possible to see him as "one of us," whoever we are.

So the showbiz elite FedEx'd him some spillage from the gross profits trough, bought a possible retirement house for him, and spiffed up an office where he could spend his ex-presidency being an executive in charge of development (meaning an endless supply of D-girls would report to him for, you know, training).

That denouement would mark a major cultural change in this country. Politics—or, to use an old-fashioned term, public service—used to be the second career of people of accomplishment. You were a successful lawyer, or (like Jesse Helms) a successful local news anchor, or (like George Murphy and Ronald Reagan) a successful mediocre actor, and politics was the world you entered in your supposedly wise maturity. Now, Bill Clinton may well spend his most distinguished years—assuming he has any distinguished years in him—as a two-bit Michael Eisner. Sure it's backward, but when a country has spent the past two decades detaching politics from respectability, it's only natural.

Much of Bill Clinton's constituency is widely reported not to hate him: union leaders, trial lawyers, the less persnickety environmentalists, African-Americans who still believe that the Democratic party has their interests at heart. Gays, always major supporters of his, seem to be trapped in an almost exquisite ambivalence about Clinton and his era. He tried to remove restrictions on their participation in the military (has anyone else noticed that the nineties have been about, among other things, people trying to get *into* places that they fought like hell to get *out of* in the sixties?), but he ended up making life in uniform harder for them. It was during his administration that Ellen DeGeneres came out, and it was on his watch that her show was canceled. Clinton appointed gay activist/meatpacking heir James Hormel to be ambassador to Luxembourg, but then was too busy with his own problems to put up much of a fight for him. It turns out Hormel had had the bad political judgment not to denounce a gay parade in which guys lampooned nuns two years before he was appointed. That's what I'd call getting spammed. (Totally off the point, can you think of anybody else in human history whose career could be summarized as "gay activist/meatpacking heir"?)

And of course, in their heart of hearts (I'm being either metaphorical or generous here), the Republican leadership doesn't hate Clinton. How could they? Sure, he hijacked some of their issues, but there are a lot more Republicans in elective office at the end of Clinton's regime than at the beginning. Plus he's managed to out-scuz Newt Gingrich, the other smart, fat narcissist our generation has hoisted to the top of the heap. For that service, as well as for his assiduous cultivation of the interest of every business larger than the Sunglass Hut, he should be named an honorary Republican.

SIDETRACK: WHAT THE DEMOCRATS HATE, WHAT THE REPUBLICANS HATE

Democrats hate Bob Barr;
Republicans hate James Carville.

Democrats hate Jesse Helms;
    Republicans hate Jesse Jackson.
Democrats hate tax cuts for the rich;
    Republicans hate targeted tax cuts.
Democrats hate school vouchers;
    Republicans hate schoolteachers.
Democrats hate Peter Duchin;
    Republicans hate Dr. Dre.

4

Other People Hated More Than Clinton

THERE WAS A TIME, late in the 1980s, when television evangelists seemed as though they'd finally used up their inexplicable reservoir of goodwill and were widely perceived to be hypocrites and charlatans. Thankfully, that aberrant moment in the history of American gullibility has passed. But, for a while, nobody's name evoked more derision and scorn than those of Jimmy (I Have Sinned) Swaggart and Jim (Here's Tammy Faye to Cry for You) Bakker—as Johnnie Cochran might have called them, the twin Jims of deception. Late-night television comedy, as always a sure barometer of the easy-reference joke, had a field day with them, their free-will gifts and offerings plummeted, and, along with the slightly less prominent but no less oleaginous Robert (I Threw Away Your Prayer Requests) Tilton, they were reviled for misusing the trust of millions.

Now they're back. All of them. Pat Robertson, who once dared to show us his naked political ambition, is back on the high road of moralistic moneygrubbing. Jerry Falwell, fresh from peddling a video accusing the Clintons of multiple murders, makes the talk-show rounds denouncing someone else's looseness with the truth. The two Jims are saving souls (in interest-bearing accounts) again, and Robert Tilton is speaking in tongues and healing the sick on many of the same stations that wouldn't sell him airtime half a decade ago. In his darker moments (does he have lighter moments now?), Bill Clinton must be asking himself, "How did they do it? How can I?"

Of course, Clinton is from the same tradition—Bible-believing Protestantism—whence they sprang, so he knows exactly how they did it. This country believes in redemption. More than half of the citizens believe in the experience of being born again, which means starting fresh; the past is not only *not* prologue, it's not even in the book. Teddy Kennedy, from a different religious tradition, still benefits greatly from this tendency, having enjoyed a fine three decades of service in the Senate while Mary Jo Kopechne's only comment continues to be "Glug."

But Teddy, like Jimmy Swaggart, knew what the rules of the redemption game were: You can be washed clean of your prior wrongdoing, but the washing liquid must include a copious amount of your own publicly shed tears. One's past is like a stubborn film of dust, removable only by the salty solvent that attends an onion's slicing. So Bill Clinton, who could muster credible lachrymosity at the tragic flooding of an ostrich farm, inexplicably decided to go authentic at the scheduled moment of redemption, the nationally televised "confession" speech on August 17, 1998. He let his anger make him look as repentant as the CEO of Archer Daniels Midland reporting on a bad soybean crop. He then became a serial apologist, serving in the process as the poster boy for the law of diminishing returns.

So evangelists are off the hated list. O.J. Simpson has undergone the reverse process—deredemption. He has surrendered that kind of fuzzy affection that surrounds retired sports stars whose accomplishments are fast receding into the memories of men with Hair Club memberships, becoming instead the reviled "Butcher of Brentwood," who can play golf only on public courses with dentists too slow of foot to desert the foursome. He, like Clinton, insists on "taking responsibility" for things without admitting he actually did them. Even so, the man is one good, tearful admission away from a monster book deal. The kind of global hatred he enjoys is devoid of the power to harm him precisely because O.J. wants nothing except what he has: to be known by every living being on the planet. In an age when John Wayne Gacy's clown paintings enjoy a thriving market, notoriety and fame are as interchangeable as Pepsi and Coke.

Car dealers, formerly the cliché of the despised, are rapidly being obsolesced by Internet car sites and no-haggling dealerships. Arabs, of course, what with the mustaches and the heavy consonants and the terrorism, are such chic objects of hatred that they're virtually the only ethnic or national group left to be cast as villains in Hollywood action epics.

More hated than any of them are lawyers. To twist an old Lincolnism, Americans must hate lawyers—that's why we made so many of them. Until the first Simpson trial, that opprobrium simmered slowly on the nation's back burner, like a fine sauce waiting for the veal to be pounded thin. Since we've been treated to the spectacle of attorneys turning briskly from getting a guilty man off to getting their own TV talk shows, America's hate affair with the legal profession has blossomed. The mere sight of F. Lee Bailey inflating like a blowfish to attempt one more televised defense of his ex-client is enough to fill any red-blooded American with the kind of murderous rage that could lead him or her to slash two people to death with a knife that nobody ever found.

Oh, yes: Bill Clinton's a lawyer. So, in addition to the obloquy aimed directly at him, he shares in theirs. He feels their pain and suffering, and I'm sure he'd like to recover damages for same.

5

People Hated So Much More Than Clinton That It's Not Even Funny

CONSIDER THE FINE MEN and women who toil ceaselessly in the interest of our right to know. Rats in the sewers of New York City plotting to feast on the eyeballs of the children in the tenements above aren't hated as thoroughly as the members of the news media. In a way this is odd, because these are, to a large extent, relatively decent, relatively intelligent, relatively good-humored guys and gals. (I'm no idiot; I get good press, and I want to keep it that way.) I worked among journalists for several different periods in my life, and much of what we blame them for is the stuff that their lunatic, ratings- or circulation-crazed bosses make them do against their own best instincts and judgments. The irony is that this is the one inside story they're never allowed to report.

That having been said, there are many good and sufficient reasons to hate the media, starting with the cliché about shooting the messenger (although everybody seems to like their FedEx guy). We blame newspeople for changing the rules over the past decade, for upending the old structure of understandings in which journalists and politicians drank together and screwed together and kept their mouths shut together, erecting instead the cage that encloses a wrestling-style battle royale. All journalists have become A. J. Weberman (the guy who used to paw through Dylan's garbage), mining the raw ore of private lives, refining it into the nightly news.

We blame journalists for this situation, even though they merely responded to our demand for more openness. The baby boomers, Bill Clinton's statistical cohort, rebelled against the cozy old system. We railed, demonstrated, and organized against the smoke-filled rooms in which professional politicians decided who was and was not fit to decide where America's draftees might be shipped off to either die or experience new, exotic syndromes. We wanted primaries instead of caucuses, never dreaming that we would end up getting long seasons of commercials that, in their quantity and crassness, would shame the adult diaper manufacturers. We wanted the truth instead of reassuring hypocrisy, and now we have more truth than we can handle, as well as hypocrisy whose hollowness offers no comfort. Sometimes, the executive class of journalism should be learning right about now, "giving the people what they want" ends up making the people very mad at you. The ratings say, "More Monica." The polls say, "We hate you for listening to the ratings."

Why else hate the media? There's the annoying habit, pioneered in television and now migrating like a computer virus into the pages of the nation's newspapers, of giving every news story its own name, logo, and (in the case of TV) theme music. "Showdown in the Gulf," "White House in Crisis," "Death of a Princess," "Birth of a Hurricane"— this is news disguised as books for the beach, light summer reading on the tube twenty-four hours a day. This ritual is all the more disquieting because of the lightning speed with which these packages are whipped together. Just imagine the frantic late-night sessions at which hastily composed "Death of a Princess" music was recorded and mixed so it could be aired even before the debris was fully removed from the tunnel: "Okay, guys, a little more urgency in the strings, let the oboes carry the sadness. *And . . .*"

This practice is not to be confused with the *-gate* mania that swept the country in the wake of Nixon's resignation. That craze can be understood, if not defended, as the primal drive of space-starved headline writers to abbreviate the day's scandal and still leave room for the newest development. I still don't know what "Whitewater" means—is it a land deal? shady billing practices at the Rose Law Firm? S&L shenanigans? all or none of the above?—but it was good, elemental, nonmelodramatic shorthand. Using the word was not an attempt to evoke an emotion, just a way of saying "that thing that Jim McDougal wanted to talk about and Susan McDougal didn't" in less than twelve letters.

It's interesting to note that virtually no one hates Bill Clinton because of Whitewater. If nine hundred FBI files turn out to have been sequestered and then thumbed through for purposes of political intimidation, that will become a reason to join the ranks of the no-longer-young ladies who tell Rupert Murdoch's publications that they fear Clinton. Intelligence files are not a plaything; if they were, J. Edgar Hoover would have used them to blackmail his nominal superiors in power. Travelgate is such small-time cronyism, even if the worst-case scenario were true, that it makes the Lewinsky affair seem portentous by comparison. The current scandal had the potential to topple a president precisely because it was simple enough for journalists to explain to the rest of us, and because, like all workaholics, they derive a strange adrenalized jolt from fantasizing about somebody else's sex life. (Ironically, the Bill-and-Monica story's very simplicity rendered it impossible to nickname: candidates like Zippergate, Monicagate, and Flytrap have all floundered, while the nearly dormant *peccadillo* has had a spectacular, and latently double-entendred, revival.)

The four words that sum up the best-known reason for hating journalists are, of course, "How do you feel?" It's the nightmare of every reporter I know to find him- or herself on live TV, thrusting a mike into the face of a father whose daughter has just been raped and murdered, or a distraught woman who's just watched her house turned into a barge by a raging flood, and to be cajoled, implored, or ordered by the producer in the earpiece to ask that question. "How do I feel? Thanks for asking, you insensitive turd. I feel like shit—how the fuck do you think I feel?" That's what the real answer to that question always is, and the first hapless interviewee who can grope through his or her despair and embarrassment to offer that response on live television will have struck a mighty blow for all mankind.

We also hate journalists because they stake out the rest of us. It's bad enough that cops and credit bureaus and Jehovah's Witnesses know where we live and regard our casas as their casas, but we've now all learned to live in dread of that unpredictable moment when our private lives dead-end, when some throwaway mention by somebody thrusts us into the penumbra of public life and our quiet streetscape turns, without warning, into a satellite-truck rodeo.

I saw a bunch of my old media friends from the O.J. Simpson civil trial hanging out one day on a Brentwood street in front of the house of Monica Lewinsky's dad, and their mood (it is another distinguished convention of media people to describe someone else's mood: "Dan, what's the mood in Moscow tonight?" "It's Russian, very Russian") combined relaxed boredom with a certain sheepishness. After all, hanging out on a residential street waiting for, at most, a five-second glimpse of somebody who's interesting only because of her recent sexual adventures is not why most of these folks went to J-school.

One reason stakeouts are infuriating is that they violate privacy and inconvenience neighbors for the sake of producing almost no news. They're ordered by assignment editors or producers who get tired, so very tired, of running the same footage of Monica hugging Bill, or of Ken Starr trudging down his driveway carrying a trashbag or a Starbucks cup. They desperately need some new tape. Of course, they could just decide not to run any video until something newsworthy happens on camera, but, yes, of course I'm dreaming. Thanks very much for the wake-up call. Those short naps are the best. Given the magic of slo-mo, which osmosed from *Hard Copy* to the evening news without so much as an ethical blink, even three seconds' worth of new video is worth the expenditure of so much time and energy, the angering of so many. How not to hate all this?

It seems a long way from the days when Redford and Hoffman wanted to play the roles of newspaper reporters. A generation of Woodward-and-Bernstein wanna-bes invaded the nation's newsrooms, for whom the five *w*'s and the *h* (who, what, where, when, why, and how) were far less interesting than the two *i*'s—investigative reporting, and I myself. Every local TV news operation that had a lease on a mobile van styled itself as the proud home of an I-Team, bumptious haircuts who barged into restaurants and demanded to see health inspection certificates, or prowled down "mean streets" in search of the shocking night-vision footage that would nail down the news, just in time for sweeps, that prostitutes still plied their trade.

By now, most people's view of the media is hopelessly skewed by the simple bad habit of watching local TV news. We all have heard the lovely couplet that encapsulates these broadcasts' approach to reporting—"If it bleeds, it leads"— but something deeper, by which I mean something shallower, is going on here. The most desired target audience for TV advertisers is young people, freshly married, starting a family, building brand loyalties that they'll carry through the rest of their consuming lives. These people, taking on frightening new burdens, finding themselves responsible for the safety and tutelage of incomprehensible bundles of joy and rage, are naturally programmed to be paranoid. If you can't be hypercautious when you've got a six-month-old relying on you, you should go back to just having dogs and cats. So local news attracts and holds these desirable viewers by preying on their genetically coded paranoia—

"Your House Could Be a Deathtrap," "Your SUV Could Kill You," "The Food the Government Doesn't Want You to Eat"—as a service to the folks who bring you Huggies.

A friend of mine, a resident of Washington, D.C., started out in the news business writing for Walter Cronkite. She was a producer for *Nightline*, Brinkley, Charlie Rose. In other words, she knows the serious news business. At the age of forty, she retired to her comfortable Georgetown town house to be a mother. When her son was six months old, she called me one day. "We've got to get out of here. We can't stay in D.C. and raise a child," she complained, her voice sharp with an edge of fear.

"Let me ask you one question," I replied. "Since you've been staying home with him, have you been watching local news?"

"Sure."

"Well, don't."

They're still in Washington, and they're fine.

The most profound reason for hating television newspeople, though, is an aesthetic one. I'm not talking about suits and haircuts here, which seem as uniform around the country as the sets that afford a fake window on the generic downtown of [your local community here]. Nor do I refer to the peculiar tendency of TV stations to hire Asian women in profusion for their newscasts (your Kaity Tongs, your Tricia Toyotas, your Wendy Tukudas), but nary an Asian man. For that matter, would Connie Chung ever have had even that half-assed shot at the coanchor chair had her first name been Charlie?

The aesthetic offense that is amputating reportorial credibility above the knees is the insistence on ersatz emoting. Reporters and anchors on television, under the hypnotic spell of mysterious consultants from the far-off land of Focusgroupia, now think it's their job not only to tell us what happened, but to indicate to us, through their intonations, their body language, their very *being*, how we should feel about the event. This is much more insidious than attempting to influence our thinking through slanted writing or jaundiced quote selection. This is much less obvious than the pathetic ad lib summations with which local newscasters button each story ("Lot there to think about, Chuck," "Too many tears in that household tonight, Candy"). This is—there's no other name for it—acting. Hideously bad acting.

I am cursed with the privilege of having a satellite dish: not the pizza-pan-sized digital dish that city councils and condo associations grudgingly tolerate, but the big analog dish that drives nosy neighbors into a microzoning fury. The difference between the two is as simple as the knowledge learned at birth by every kid of the garment trade: The little dish is like buying retail, the big dish is like buying wholesale. It's on their big dishes that networks and local stations receive feeds from their anchors and reporters at remote locations. Watch these guys and gals, as I do, rehearsing and re-taking, long after they've got the text correct and the shot looks good, still working on getting the oomph of the particular emotion—sadness, great sadness, ironic sadness—that they're trying to convey. It's like open-mike night at mime camp. Watch, as I have, Tom Brokaw do a retake of his conclusion to a cute filler story ("Of course, who will have the last laugh?") just to get a little more chuckle into his voice. "Phony" doesn't begin to describe the meretriciousness of these performances. Even if you had the biggest tits in the world, you couldn't get on *Baywatch* with acting this bad. Yet it's now peddled to us as "reporting."

Again, you can't blame the perpetrators. Like the Nazi soldiers, they're only following orders. Which only makes things worse. Like the lawyers who can wriggle off any hook by saying, "Hey, it's not my job to ask my client if he's guilty," the excuse to which these people are entitled only makes them more loathsome. But newspeople aren't (yet) trained as actors. They're bad at it. And nothing is less believable than bad acting. This is why their credibility has sunk so low.

Most Americans may not analyze why they find newspeople so unbelievable, ascribing the problem instead to some imputed bias. I just did the analysis for you. You're welcome. That's why I get the medium-sized bucks. Take it from me—the only bias most TV newspeople have is the extreme one in favor of keeping their jobs.

6

One Reason Why People
Should Hate Clinton

A NYTIME POLITICIANS FEEL EMBOLDENED—
or, as they and their defenders say, required—
to make pronouncements on morality, our society
is in trouble. Not because of the perceived immo-
rality that forces them to rush to their thesauruses
and word processors, but because we need moral
guidance from politicians like we need medical ad-
vice from the *Car Talk* guys.

These are, after all, people who've regarded the
possibility of spending life shaking hands, asking
for money, and having horrible things said about
them every two or four years as an agreeable career
choice. It's bad enough to hear them tell us in
tones of studied piety why a new dam in their district isn't pork but mental health clinics for the

homeless are. But when Sen. Joseph Lieberman (D-Con Man) set aside his previous crusade with Bill Bennett (demanding that Time Warner stop distributing gangsta rap records and stick to its more morally uplifting business of releasing luxuriantly violent movies) and took to the Senate floor to deliver his jeremiad on Bill Clinton's "immoral" behavior, it was Katy-bar-the-door for all the pols who look longingly at Jerry Falwell's gig.

In the lifetimes of the youngest among us, we've heard wrenching debates about who our role models should be. Candidates considered, then found wanting, have included Bart Simpson, Charles Barkley, and Michael Milken. And now there's a race to the Senate podium or the well of the House to pronounce the president unfit for the moral guidance that our children, bereft of Bart and Barkley, so desperately need. The following point would seem obvious were it not being drowned out by the caterwauling of the suddenly pious: A society that seeks moral leadership for its children from cartoon characters, basketball players, and elected glad-handers is in terrible trouble. How about, just to take an example from the primitives and the pagans, taking moral leadership from the older and wiser among us? Nah, that's a bad look, with the wrinkles and the teeth and the liver spots. Better to assume that people who've spent every moment of their waking lives ignoring the moral dimension of their activities have something uplifting to tell us, some sterling example to set for the kiddies.

As unbearable as all this is, it will get worse. We will be lectured on righteousness by the takers of corporate and union largesse (the senators from Archer Daniels Midland, the congressmen from AFSCME), hear ringing declamations of a need for national sacrifice by the enjoyers of junkets (golf is the mother's milk of politics), endure untold paeans to purity by men and women whose tree-shakers are busy in the boiler rooms downstairs (at least until the random-dialing computers take over). The national nausea that will ensue can fairly be laid at the trouser-tousled feet of Bill Clinton.

7

People Who Should
Hate Clinton

Pᴇᴏᴘʟᴇ ᴡʜᴏ sʜᴏᴜʟᴅ ʜᴀᴛᴇ Clinton: Elected
Democrats. Democrats who want to be elected.
Democrats who work for elected Democrats. People who raise money for Democrats. You get the
point.

I haven't talked to my two friends who are
Democratic congressmen since the Paula Jones
lawsuit metastasized, so I can only go by what we
can call the Matt Drudge rule (if it seems true, it
is). It leads me to believe that any Democratic
officeholder who doesn't hate Bill Clinton is either
facing term limits or really does want to spend more
time with his family. The man from Arkansas took
them along on his roller-coaster ride of tempting
fate and then rescuing himself, a serial adventure in

which seat belts were no match for centrifugal force, especially at election time.

Serious political junkies should hate Bill Clinton for sabotaging the chance to talk about anything but him (a narcissist's dream: imagine how overjoyed O.J. must have been to have cable during his trial). Of course, MSNBC would have gone under by now if their daily diet had had to be "Kosovo in Crisis" or "Investigating the IMF." As far as I'm concerned, every time Bill Clinton has said, "I just want to get back to doing what the people sent me here to do," I want to scream back at the offending loudspeaker, "Schmuck, this *is* what we sent you there to do—star in an entertaining sex scandal!"

Feminists should hate Clinton because he has forced many of them to defend exactly the kind of behavior they condemned out of hand when Republicans engaged in it.

Frankly, I was never that convinced of the fairness of a body of law that said a woman's sexual history was always out of bounds and a man's sexual history was always fair game. We saw the rigor of the previous style of law in action during the trial of the aforementioned Mr. Simpson: Judge Ito, in one of his few decisions not swayed by the consideration of what would impress the celebrities visiting his chamber, refused to let the prosecution prove its case by introducing evidence of O.J.'s previous bad behavior toward Nicole. Had the charge against him been not double murder but sexual harassment, all that earlier stuff would have flooded in. For the slow learners among us, this double standard grew to grotesque proportions during Marv Albert's trial, when he stood accused of looting Frederick's of Hollywood and being grand marshal of Wigstock while his alleged victim's very name was kept quiet until he copped a plea. Clinton's case has made a whole new group of people—liberals—see how unfair that particular thumb on the scale of justice turns out to be.

Prosecutors should *really* hate Clinton. In one of the truest statements to be televised during the whole mess, Republican lawyer Joseph di Genova told MSNBC, or CNBC, or *Saturday Night Live*, that "Ken Starr's office isn't using any tactics not being used by every prosecutor's office in every city in this country every day." That's also one of the scariest statements. Twenty years of the war on drugs and the RICO statutes against organized crime have emboldened America's prosecutors to use everything but electrodes on the genitals in the pursuit of their prey. This was their little secret as long as the prey were largely people whose language or skin color ensured that the only television network they'd ever be depicted on was either Univision or UPN. But Clinton, by drawing Ken Starr into using those tactics on a high-profile white man, has exposed the game. I wouldn't look for him to be man of the year at the DA convention anytime soon.

But, just to drive the point home once more, these are people whose hatred has been assiduously earned by postinaugural behavior. Congressional Democrats felt betrayed just as soon as Dick Morris convinced Clinton to treat them like so many used Accu-Jacks. But the hatred that needs explanation is that which attached to Bill Clinton's head before it turned fully gray, which already surrounded him like a toxic fog while we were still learning not to say the name Bush after the title "President."

8

So Why Do Some People
Really, Really Hate Clinton?

I HAVE A FRIEND, a right-wing comedy writer, who has always genially despised both Clintons. His reason, or so he says (I don't think he's getting money from Richard Mellon Scaife—hell, I don't think *I* am, but who knows for sure?), is the considerable amount of self-righteousness they exuded about the period that preceded their ascension to office. To my friend—let's call him Victor—the Reagan-Bush years were an epoch of triumph. The end of the cold war, the tax cuts, the—gee, I can't imagine what else he might be thinking of as even possible triumphs, but that's his reading. In the Clinton rhetoric of the first campaign and the early first term, though, the 1980s had been a shameful era of selfishness, greed, and neglect of social priorities. My friend—let's call him Lex— may not always discern a truckload of hypocrisy whenever self-righteousness rears its well-coiffed head, but he snuffled it out here like a pig in truffle country. In the wake of revelations about Hillary's fabulous touch with the commodities market, he turned out to be right. *Now* who's self-righteous?

(Hatred of Hillary has been a harmony vocal part to the anti-Clinton chorus all along. She's a strong, proud, smart, meddlesome woman who's always been the true liberal in the family. Rumors about the "arrangement" at the heart of the Clinton marriage are not kind to her, any more than Dick Morris was when he opined on a Los Angeles radio breakfast show that she might well be a lesbian. He later told me on Fox News that "that was a hypothetical"; presumably he was talking about a conceptual Hillary Clinton, not the one we know. Like a Hollywood producer chafing at the way all the attention goes to the actors and the director, she has insisted on her face time. She has been reported to be the reason the Paula Jones suit wasn't settled for so long, and the reason the post-grand-jury-appearance speech by Clinton was so combative. Tough chicks haven't played well since *Happy Days*.)

The tone of self-righteousness has persisted in Clintonian rhetoric. Here's a recent presidential quote about his discovery that he had intractable opponents: "You know, sometimes when you try to effect that kind of transformation, you know you're going to provoke a reaction. I didn't dream it would be quite as profound as it has been—this reaction."

Transformation! *That's* what he's been taking us through. To be honest with you, I don't feel that different, and I look, if anything, a little worse than when all this started. But creeping hair loss is a kind of a transformation, I guess.

To be fair, Bill Clinton has transformed the national debate. Just as Nixon press secretary Ron Ziegler's "Contrition is bullshit!" quote marked the first time that bovine ordure had been referred to colloquially on the front pages of the nation's newspapers, Clinton has made the media safe for ejaculate and cigars with a certain flavor. Just to see the Washington press corps feign prudish disgust over sexual activities far less unusual than those engaged in by, say, the typical British member of Parliament (one such worthy was found dead, hanging by the neck, an orange in his mouth and a plastic bag over his head) has been transforming. These are the same people who regale each other at

Georgetown dinner parties with the latest, hottest rumors about the private lives of politicians high and low, but keep predicting a "yuck factor" among the great unwashed when we learn about the cigar or the macadamia nuts. Actually, the real transformation being experienced by the Washington press corps is the realization that they no longer have these juicy stories all to themselves. We can all regale each other over dinner with this stuff now. The challenge for us is to skip dinner and get straight to the dirt.

TOP SEXUAL LIES NOT TOLD BY CLINTON

1. Terry Dolan, who ran the right-wing NCPAC that funded many Republican candidates who ran against Democrats for being soft on gay rights, died of AIDS, a closeted gay man.
2. Ronald Reagan's first gubernatorial term in California narrowly

---

avoided a sex scandal when, at a
Lake Tahoe summit, he fired aides
suspected of being gay.

3. Henry Hyde's five-year affair with a
married woman, begun when he
was forty-one, was described by
him, after it was revealed in an
online magazine, as "a youthful
indiscretion."

But self-righteousness, while it may offend the
tender sensibilities of the *artistes* on the right like
my friend Toby, isn't really the basis of the boiling,
seething, festering, suppurating hatred that's been
aimed at the president since he and Al Gore boo-
gied to "Don't Stop (Thinkin' About Tomorrow)"
on election night 1992. So what is?

Bill Clinton grew up southern and poor. He
ended up president and, if decidedly not rich himself, at least palling around Malibu and the Hamptons with the richerati, eating their blinis and

drinking their Puligny-Montrachet. To put it bluntly, he's a traitor to his class. Now, I'm real, real sorry—sorrier than the president, in actual fact—to bring up the word *class*. It's been excised from the acceptable political vocabulary, except in the limited usage of right-wingers when they accuse liberals of inciting "class warfare"—a charge that means it's okay for rich people to vote their economic interests but it's not all right to encourage poor people to do so. Merely saying the word brings to mind images of bearded, smelly Marxists who want all of us to wear Mao jackets and drive Yugos.

Being perhaps the most talented group of humans on the planet when it comes to euphemisms, we Americans have dispensed with the word *class* but continue to talk about the same subject in the pseudoscientific patois of "demographics." We know as well as we know our own phone numbers the magical age-and-income group sought by big advertisers, the middle and upper-middle 18-to-34s, or, in the case of more tolerant marketers, the 18-to-49s—a preference that is pandered to by all our commercial media, a class preference that dictates the nature of most of our popular culture. But it's okay, that's just "demographics." You may have even seen the more detailed breakdowns of the buying styles of different groups—the "early adopters" of new technology, for example, who are merely a gussied-up version of an older concept, the "nouveaux riches."

Unfortunately, wishing that we were a classless society does not make us one. When James Carville uttered his immortal crack about dragging a piece of currency through a trailer park, he was not offering us a commentary on land-use patterns. He was suggesting that the self-styled elites, and all who had hopes of eventually so styling themselves, should look down on trashy ol' Paula Jones and, by extension, should disbelieve her charge of gubernatorial flashing. Conversely, whenever you hear the compound adjective "chardonnay-sipping" applied to Bill Clinton's supporters, the intended response is not a thoughtful meditation on the pros and cons of heavy oaking, but a gut-level reaction against the airs of a class above the target audience, whose wine of preference, if any, the speaker assumes will come in a box.

Yes, I know, we're the most meritocratic society this side of Iceland, with an astounding amount of social mobility. You can be born poor and disadvantaged in this great country and still grow up to be Kathie Lee Gifford. This is a good thing, and ignoring this reality is one reason (in addition to perpetrating a depressing series of mass slaughters) why the Communist Party never made it big here.

In general, the nonrich in America tend merely to envy the rich rather than to want them dead and available for immediate pillaging, but something wacky does happen when a person from your group rises far above the rest of you. Two wacky things, usually: The person often forgets, except for ceremonial/rhetorical purposes, the humble nature of his origins, and those he left behind often end up looking for proof that he's "putting on airs" as an excuse to hate his guts. This may be less true in Phoenix, more true in Little Rock.

The South, I don't have to kill any more trees to remind you, is the most conservative part of the country. It's also in many ways closer to our British roots than the cosmopolitan Northeast, the Germanic-Scandinavian Midwest, or the surfers' West Coast. You can hear it in the way Virginian Pat Robertson pronounces the word *out*—taken in isolation, that sound could make you think he was Canadian (It's a trivial dream, but it's my dream). British culture still maintains a terrible antimobility bias. The lone flower is always pulled back down to the surrounding earth. With the exception of recent recruits to the ethos of American ambition like Atlanta and Charlotte, a lot of the South still shares that bias. It is a bias in favor of community and continuity and comformity, against initiative and individuality.

Just compare Bill Clinton's opposition to that of the last son of the South to occupy the White House, Jimmy Carter. Nobody hated Carter, although he got the usual amount of derision (younger readers are advised to type the following phrases into their search engines: "killer rabbit" and "lust in my heart"). He was humble to a fault, he was pious to a fault. Hell, he was faultless to a fault. The fanciest person he ever hung around with was his wife, and she was from the same hometown as he—Plains. Sure, he rose high, but he never forgot his roots. In fact, there were clods of Georgia peanut-farming soil all over his roots. His enemies charged him with excessive attention to detail, with inaction in the face of spiraling prices and interest rates, and with inability to get the hostages out of Iran. They never charged him with unsolved murders back in Georgia.

Bill Clinton, on the other hand, brings down a northern girl to marry. Sure, he cheated on her, but she's still a northerner. Then, after turning his back on one of the South's most cherished institutions, the military, he goes off to Oxford like some rich guy's son, and before you know it, he's getting two-hundred-dollar haircuts in an airplane, for God's sake. He hangs with Streisand and Spielberg and Geffen and that designer in the Hamptons— people who are either rich, Jewish, or gay. If that isn't putting your thumb in the eye of rock-bottom Dixie, what is?

Obviously, some of this class jumping is a political necessity: You party with the people who can put the most dollars in the kitty (Hey, Ms. Kanchanalak, how ya doin'?), but over time, Clinton visibly and notoriously has come to dig the high life, to the point where the most popular report about his pending ex-presidency has him moving to Malibu and commuting to Dream-Works SKG, as opposed to, say, building houses for the poor, or, to take the other extreme, renting himself out like Gerald Ford for ten grand a pop.

Even Dick Morris, the panpolitical adviser turned opinionator for the Murdoch News Channel and the man who made sucking the toes of a prostitute seem suddenly sleazy, picked up on the regional perception of Clinton as a class traitor. In 1995, Bill and Hillary wanted to vacation on

Martha's Vineyard, where their adopted demographic mates summer. It was Morris who insisted that they pack off instead to a more proletarian holiday in backcountry Wyoming. Only after Clinton was safely reelected did he decide it was safe to hobnob with the swells again.

(Incidentally, is there any real difference between sucking a prostitute's toes and being a news analyst for Rupert Murdoch? Yes; in the sessions with the hooker, nobody got screwed.)

In fact, Clinton got the class thing exactly backward. His way of connecting with his roots was in his choice of foods and sex partners, while his politics and his selection of acquaintances were more aspirationally upscale than the *Robb Report*. In a way, putting on airs is all about being aspirationally upscale as opposed to appearing organically, relaxedly, authentically upper-class. Jack Kennedy, though he needed some nudging by Jackie, gave off the aura of having been born the type of person who'd actually want Pablo Casals playing in his White House. His adoring protégé Bill Clinton is a rock-and-roll arriviste, hoping people won't notice that, at the Kiri Te Kanawa recital, he's humming Fleetwood Mac under his breath.

The most yuppified action he ever took, of course, occurred long before the word *yuppie* was invented, but it marked Clinton as an antisoutherner: he dodged the draft. Don't get me wrong—in my book (and this is my book), there's nothing bad about refusing to let oneself become just another shipment of boneless chuck fed into the industrial-grade Cuisinart of a stupid war. Frankly, I'd be reluctant to vote for anybody who did serve in Vietnam, purely on the grounds of questions about his intelligence.

But Clinton did his draft dodging the way he did his White House adultery, half-assed, leaving the door open a crack to discourage suspicion, looking over his shoulder to see if he was maintaining his "political viability." The military class, revered in the South as the essence of true manhood, has long been reported to despise their commander in chief, and, since southerners have big families, you can just imagine the postcards sizzling home from the PX.

But even in the American South, betraying your class isn't enough to earn you the fervid animosity Bill Clinton has found clinging to himself like jellyfish parts. After all, Rush Limbaugh lords it over his largely lumpen listenership, bragging about his expensive cigars, his nights in the George Bush White House, his capacious Manhattan apartment (if he can find enough space there, he can find it anywhere), and the dittoheads revere him for it. Well, sure—if you stay conservative, the crackers will cut you more cultural slack. And, judging by the briefest skimming of his biography, Rush (né Rusty) Limbaugh never was dirt-poor southern. He was small-town border-state shabby respectable. Bill Clinton did betray his origins in an even more incendiary way: It's possible to say that, in the view of the traditional southern white male, he was a traitor to his sex.

Both Jimmy Carter and Lyndon Johnson were married, let's recall, to smart, ambitious women. Neither of them dared to brag about that fact during their election campaigns; neither of them had the audacity to boast, as Clinton did, that "you buy one, you get one free." Even though Carter and LBJ were around during the very early emergence in our culture of the strong woman, they knew that, as president, you don't want to be seen leaning on one. In fact, of course, plenty of presidents have done exactly that. Woodrow Wilson comes to mind, and Ronald Reagan comes at least to my mind, if not, at this point, to his. It was always part of the game to pretend that the guy in the house was doing all the heavy lifting, much as it is in homes across America. Women have been putting up with this little charade for eons, and they'll keep putting up with it until they bring home a larger slice of the bacon than their man does. Maybe even after that.

Given the fragility of the male ego, *especially* after that.

Such amiable pretense went out the window with the Clintons (again with the boomer openness). Hillary was given tasks, responsibilities, bailiwicks. So were a lot of other bright, talented women who were equipped with enough foresight to deduct Social Security taxes from their nanny's checks. The seeming collegiality of this administration— so many of Clinton's sentences begin with "Hillary and I" or "Al Gore and I"—made it easier to stare into the abyss of impeachment and conviction. If we bought one and got one free, maybe we could keep one and get rid of one, and still have . . . one.

Bill Clinton gave women plenty of jobs and— come on, we can all finish this sentence together. But he also did what red-blooded American men, especially southerners, aren't supposed to do: He hid behind women's skirts. Hillary saved his ass when Gennifer Flowers surfaced in the 1992 campaign by going on *60 Minutes* and vouching for him while denying that she was "standing by my man." Of course not; she was sitting. Susan Mc-Dougal put her jailed, chained body between Clinton and Ken Starr for two years, living out old Sam Arkoff B-movie fantasies in the process. Betty Currie's role, as revealed in Starr's recent opus, *Harold Robbins Goes to Law School,* was to facilitate the TBJC (ten blow jobs and a cigar). She was the housemother, and Clinton was the fraternity of one. Then, when cornered, he assumed the position of hiding behind her reputation for church-going probity, a reputation he had just helped to destroy.

Most crucially, Bill Clinton was hoping to hide behind Monica's pantsuit. If he ever bothered to war-game this thing out one move ahead, he must have assumed that she would continue to deny that the TBJC ever took place, even to the extremity of landing her own ass in the slammer. In other words (and here's why maybe we need a chess player in the White House instead of a hearts player), Clinton was betting that, even after Lewinsky threatened him with disclosure in order to get her dream job, even after he knew she had lied to him about keeping the affair quiet—she had told one person for every blow job, plus a bonus person, for a total of eleven—she would *still* stick with her false affidavit or refuse to testify. At the spectacle of this guy basing the very survival of his presidency on the courage (or lovesick foolishness) of a twenty-five-year-old girl, you can just hear the low roar from truck stops and Waffle Houses: "Be a *man*, for chrissake!"

9

Is That All You Have?
If Not, Get on with It!
And Free Kevin Mitnick!

SORRY. THE COMPUTER IN charge of the chapter headings appears to have been hacked. One moment, please.

10

One More Reason People
Hate Bill Clinton

REMEMBER MY PREMISE, NOW: Most of Clinton's die-hard nonsupporters are based in the South. What is it they hate even more, in the depths of their antebellum hearts, than highfalutin ex-rednecks and uppity women? Here's a clue: No poor white boy who came back home pretending to be a Harvard man ever found his highfalutin ass hanging from a tree. Bill Clinton has been perceived as a traitor to his race.

African-Americans have been among his most steadfast supporters. That can be explained partly by their historical loyalty to a Democratic Party that every once in a while (usually around election time) remembers to do something good for them.

Newt Gingrich, during his full-of-himself phase, regularly made noises that scared hell out of most people who did not yet have their own modems, Volvos, and Dolby Surround sound systems. So black voters made their commitment to Clinton and stuck with it.

He, in turn, has been—given his tendency not to take most issues he cares about "to completion," to borrow a Starrism—consistent, believable, even heartfelt on issues of race. He did spend some political capital campaigning against the repeal of affirmative action in California. He did pepper his administration with substantial numbers of minority appointees. He did really try to have "a national dialogue about race," although it also might have occurred to him that a year of public conversation on so divisive a subject would have served as a mighty nice distraction from subjects like Paula Jones and Chinese campaign funds.

Yes, Lyndon Johnson called for a war on poverty, but, just as FDR was smart enough to realize that Social Security had to cover the well-to-do along with the poor in order to avoid the stigma of a welfare program, LBJ never missed a chance to emphasize that far more white people were poor than black. He knew that a program stigmatized as race-based welfare, which the war on poverty eventually became, was destined to fail, which it eventually did.

Only Clinton, among our recent southern presidents, was consistently forthright on race. This seems to be one of the rare subjects on which authenticity was allowed to peep through the meticulously crafted facade. Not even Dick Morris could get him off the race kick. Bill Clinton was a white southerner who had grown up in the latter years of Jim Crow, who had seen his local political heroes like Bill Fulbright get ensnared in the tangled web of race politics, who knew that the only way out of the briar patch was to just get out, to have a great national back-turning on a century of race baiting and much, much worse.

Because most normal Americans have race on their minds these days only when they start thinking about what school their kids are going to attend, much of this consistency and forthrightness got lost in the noise. But two audiences paid very close attention to Clinton's stance as a white southerner determined to help erase the great stain: African-Americans, who rewarded him with even greater loyalty, and certain white southerners, who rewarded him with the kind of white-hot, self-perpetuating hatred generated nowhere else in this society.

Here's a little story about how goofy the race thing can be. We all know Compton, California, today as the home of Bill Bennett's favorite form of music, gangsta rap. But as late as the 1950s, Compton was a plain-vanilla suburb of LA. When the changeover came—and, as it did in much of urban America, it came quickly—it occurred to some of the white liberal teachers at Compton High School (now almost all black) that the school's team nickname should be changed to something less prone to misinterpretation than it was at the time: the Tarbabes. Don't ask me what the original meaning of the name was, but it seemed bizarre in the extreme to have fifteen black kids run out on the basketball court while the PA announcer boomed, "Let's welcome the Tarbaaaabes!" This was at a time when political correctness was beginning to demand that at schools with no discernible Native American populations, like Stanford, nicknames should be changed to expunge unfortunate echoes of the past ("Want some blankets? No, no smallpox on 'em, why do you ask?"). So the Indians became the Cardinal, although why Washington's football team hasn't gone from the Redskins to the Multicoloredskins, I don't quite know.

Back at Compton High, the student body devoured and debated the topic of the team's nickname for weeks. The way it seemed to break down at the time was that the poorer black kids, or those who'd recently come from rural areas, hated the name and wanted it changed, while the middle-class college-prep black kids refused to surrender a tradition they somehow valued just to erase what someone else thought was an insult. Tarbabes it stayed. If you insist on being pedantic and drawing a lesson from the episode, how about this: White liberals should take a good, deep breath before trying to substitute their own judgment for that of those they see as victims. (Taking a deep breath was the prescription the Clintons and their supporters used to give everyone in the early days of the scandal, as in "Let's all take a deep breath and wait for the facts to come in." I suppose the presumption was that the president's troubles could all be ascribed to an epidemic of shallow breathing.)

This race thing can be wacky, unpredictable, troublesome. We are far away from the time when the issues were simple—should black people have the vote, or should they be sponges for Bull Connor's fire hoses?—and even then, white politicians had to be dragged kicking and screaming into taking public positions on them. Today, academicians hurl statistical thunderbolts at each other that either prove or disprove the hypothesis that affirmative action programs do more harm than good. It's a rare political figure who'd voluntarily stride into that bog. Bill Clinton did.

But let's be fair—fairness, after all, being the chief Democratic virtue, just as freedom is the chief Republican one. Let's be fair to the white southerners who appear to be at the core of the Clinton haters. They have observed, correctly, that this president has been consistent in his support of, and by, one other constituency besides African-Americans: those who make their living through international trade. Bill Clinton spent political capital as if it were Canadian money when the time came to gain passage of laws, like NAFTA and fast-track, that would enlarge the ambit of global capitalism and enhance the free flow of profit-seeking dollars. In Minneapolis or Baltimore, that policy can be debated on the merits: whether free trade produces a net job loss or gain, whether it's been a union killer, whether Michael Jordan really should go visit a Nike plant in Vietnam and smell the fumes that envelop the kids who work there.

But in the South, and in parts of the mountain West, this all looks very different. Remember, in the aftermath of the Oklahoma City bombing, how we got that brief burst of interest in the militia movement? I was working in a play in New York at the time. The local paper had printed the frequency of a shortwave radio station targeted at militia members (there's your narrowcasting), and I used to entertain myself on my twenty-block walk to the theater each night by listening to various raspy voices spinning out monologues that would have taxed the attention spans of PBS executives. No production values, no music or sound effects, just lengthy diatribes on the unbroken line of worldwide Masonic-Jewish conspiracy dating back to, roughly, the invention of water. Of course, militia members don't have a lot of other entertainment alternatives: the choice for an evening's amusement would be to listen to this stuff or sit and watch the cabin rot.

This is not to say that, once you buy into the minimalist aesthetic and the paranoid worldview, these broadcasts can't be fascinating. There's been a great deal of bemoaning recently about the decline of the narrative sense in American writing, not only in the movies, where plots are merely clotheslines upon which to hang explosions, but also in novels that substitute attitude for story. Well, you want sustained narrative flow that takes you through five hundred years of European and American history, that knits together more disparate characters and locales than E. L. Doctorow ever dreamed of? Check out your shortwave paranoids. There's narrative galore. Nobody can weave together seemingly unconnected details more compellingly than a studious, intelligent paranoid.

These listening experiences reminded me that there exist in this country people whose view of those engaged in international trade and finance goes way beyond dim. They believe such activities are the work of the devil, and they look for the marks of the devil in the most arcane places (best places for the devil to leave his mark, I'd say). You get my drift on this? These are people who make Lyndon LaRouche's accusations that the queen of England is an international drug smuggler sound downright moderate. Do these people exist anywhere outside the world of the militia—say, just to take an example out of thick air, within a twenty-mile radius of Parker Dozhier's bait shack in Arkansas, where David Hale used to hang out? Well, you won't find me poking around that vicinity, but you're welcome to hie yourself down there and inquire of the neighbors, "Hey, what's your view on black folks and international bankers?" (Helpful hint: Try not to be driving a car with New York or California plates.)

By these lights, Bill Clinton is a tool of a race-mixing, international-financial-conspiracy-running Supreme Evil One. When you think you're up against an enemy like that, mounting a five-year campaign that accuses him of murder, drug running, or even things he may actually have done doesn't seem so maniacally extreme. It may not only be *not* overdoing it, it may be the only way to save humanity. Do the people who hate Clinton this fervently and viscerally think there may be a Nobel prize in it for them? Are you kidding? They probably think the Nobel committee is in on the conspiracy.

11

So Should We Hate the People
Who Hate Clinton, or What?

Interesting question. Glad I thought of it.
Look, I'm a child of the sixties. As is Bill
Clinton. Which is, by the way, one final reason
why people hate him. Who thought, in the heady
days of Haight-Ashbury, when our idea of an in-
novative social program was free concerts in the
park, that the first emblematic figure of our generation would be the most equivocal semi–dope
smoker, semi–draft dodger, semi–free lover ever to
be part of our age group? As Pat Buchanan tried to
tell us at the 1992 Republican convention, America
is involved in a culture war. Bill Clinton, who, had
he been a woman of his generation, would have
burned half his bra, is the de facto leader of whatever side of that war Robert Bork opposes—even

though, ultimately, he appears to have been drafted into that role.

Linda Tripp, who has steadfastly insisted she had no political agenda in starting the avalanche with a trip to Radio Shack, may have been telling the truth. But she clearly had a cultural agenda. She was widely reported to have been disgusted when, after the propriety of the Bush White House, the Clinton gang came in with their jeans and their sneakers and, in the case of George Stephanopoulos, his "dirty hair." Hearing Linda Tripp talk about the Clinton White House is like hearing our parents talk about the Rolling Stones. To misquote von Clausewitz, politics is the generational war by other means.

We are told by nostalgic conservatives (shouldn't nostalgia be the official emotion of conservatives?) that Ronald Reagan so respected the Oval Office that he never took his jacket off while he was within its confines. For some reason, that image seems to persist in their memories far better than the trading of arms for hostages. It's a cultural statement, pure and simple. The grown-ups knew how to behave in the executive mansion. The kids turned it into Animal House. Incidentally, I have a fairly vivid memory of one of those jackets, and I know why he didn't take it off: One of his aides might have attempted to put it back on the horse.

Sure, it's ironic with cherries on top that Bill Clinton, whose kinship with his generation was always more chronological than ideological or behavioral, became the receptacle for all the pent-up I-told-you-so-ing of a generation he was so eager to ape (he said, in a seldom-remembered remark shortly after taking office, that he'd learned much from Reagan's presidency; little did we know that what he'd studied was the latter's flair for genially plausible mendacity). As in so many other ways, Clinton has fallen short. Reagan was America's best supporting man, the leading man's best friend; Clinton has become America's stand-in, his cheeseball draft evasion substituting for the draft-card-burning lovers of Ho Chi Minh, his noninhaling experiment on foreign shores standing in for the empty-eyed acidheads begging for spare change on our street corners, his furtive fumbling for hallway blow jobs standing in for John and Yoko naked in bed on the world's TV screens.

But, as I said, I'm a child of the sixties. Just as the civil-rights veterans forgave the once-fearsome George Wallace (much easier to forgive when he was sitting in a wheelchair, shaking with Parkinson's, scary as a beetle on its back), I say we should love-bomb the Clinton haters. Stick a flower in the barrel of Richard Mellon Scaife's rifle. Flash a peace sign at Larry Klayman. Give Larry Nichols a state job, for God's sake. Buy some night crawlers from Parker Dozhier. Help Ken Starr get back his lost deanship in Malibu. Get Linda Tripp the name of Paula Jones's cosmetic surgeon. Their motives, as I've tried to discern them, may have been strikingly less than noble. But their efforts have helped us see more clearly a president whose brilliance and cunning could not keep him from lapses of judgment and acts of recklessness that, had they happened during the cold war, would have made for one very scary movie.

A lifelong middler and diddler miscast as an avatar of radical globalism, who has arrayed against him a collection of cranks and bigots donning the raiment of moralists—this masquerade, too frightening for Halloween, looks like a Mardi Gras float that veered off Canal Street and lumbered its way up to Pennsylvania Avenue. Even so, in the goofy way that life works, William Jefferson Clinton got the enemies he deserved. Many of us do.

Epilogue: Why Clinton Should Hate Us

HE WAS ONLY TRYING to please. Sure, a lot of times he was only trying to please himself, but on other occasions he only wanted to please us, to tell us what we wanted to hear, to make us feel good about feeling good about him. And how did we repay him?

We gave him our highest office at a time when history said its chief work was to revisit the boring old ground of the Balkans, which we didn't even care about the first time it set off a world war. Then we let an insane Supreme Court decide that, sure, a sexual harassment case could go on a nation-wide talent search for Jane Does without distraction to a sitting president.

Given what we now know about his proclivity

for, in the Starr report's elegant term, finishing himself off, there's a poetry to the justice here. But what about us? Historians at their most airily distant like to say that the country usually gets the president it deserves. Could Clinton fairly blame his lack of commitment on ours? "I tried," he might be saying to us now, "I tried to give you what you said you wanted." Certainly he fine-tuned every part of his increasingly tiny agenda (school uniforms, childproof caps for Viagra bottles) in constant consultation with pollsters. But then the politics of both sides are calibrated in exactly the same way, to push the buttons of those few people who still see fit to answer personal and political questions from strangers over the phone. "I didn't invent this game," a more candid Clinton would tell us. "I just played the hell out of it. Trent Lott didn't get blamed for listening to Dick Morris; why was I?"

Both our politics and our entertainment have been hobbled by aping the decision-making process of advertisers. Advertising, after all, is something we'd just as soon avoid, so polling and focus groups have been designed to find strategies to evade our avoidance, ways to get around our resistance to unrelenting sales pitches. But entertainment and politics are normally significant parts of the lifeblood of a culture, messages of human drama and comedy and community leadership that humans would not usually seek to avoid. The canniness of using advertisers' strategies to craft ever-more-irresistible entertainments and political messages has paid off in absolutely interchangeable TV shows and movies, and a voter turnout rate plummeting toward zero.

I divide my time these days between California and Louisiana. In California, where the spirit of reform has blown like a desiccating Santa Ana over the fields of politics for nearly a century, public life is boring, the players are known only to each other, and more and more money is spent chasing fewer and fewer voters. In Louisiana, corruption is as endemic as crawfish, politics is a lively spectator sport, a contest between the rogues and the rascals (the bumper stickers for Gov. Edwin Edwards's campaign against David Duke said, "Vote for the crook—it's important!"). The campaign finance reforms of the post-Watergate era have given us, instead of CREEP checks being laundered through Mexico, Chinese government checks being laundered through a Buddhist temple in suburban LA. Onward and upward.

Alone among the nations of the world, this

country sited its political capitals in hick towns, removed and protected from the corrupting influences of commerce and the arts. The uniquely American search for purity in politics may have found its final resting place in a hallway just off the Oval Office. "Look, you ingrates," Clinton should be saying to us right about now. "I'm giving you a punctuation mark to a century of pointless reform. You guys can't fairly insist that we pols spend our youth and early middle age shimmying up the greasiest pole in the country and somehow emerge on top with clean hands. If you folks want saints running your government," Bill Clinton should tell us, if he dared, "why don't y'all just move to heaven?"

Index

ABOUT THE AUTHOR

HARRY SHEARER has produced an inimitable and irreverent body of work in every major entertainment genre. He is a creator and star of the seminal "rockumentary" on the dinosaur rock bands, *This Is Spinal Tap*. His voice brings to life many of the denizens of *The Simpsons* universe. He has appeared in such movie blockbusters as *Godzilla* and *The Truman Show*. He is a former writer and cast member on *Saturday Night Live*. He has been a commentator on *ABC's World News Now*, a writer for the e-zine *Slate*, and a columnist for the *Los Angeles Times Magazine*. He has appeared as a guest star on the prime-time hits *ER, Chicago Hope, Miami Vice, Friends,* and *Murphy Brown*. And his critically acclaimed radio program *Le Show* is now entering its sixteenth year.

Shearer is also a multimedia artist. He has created several acclaimed exhibits of public figures captured on satellite in eerie silence while waiting for television coverage to begin—including *Wall of Silence*, and installation at MOCA revealing key figures from the O.J. Simpson trial in their *least* mediagenic moments. He made his first foray into the world of book publishing with the collection of essays *Man Bites Town*, which the *New York Times* called "comic social satire of a very high order."

No one can say what, or who, will arise next from the acting-writing-directing-always-whirring imagaination of Harry Shearer—least of all Shearer, who finds himself in the service of his creations.

A Note on The Library of Contemporary Thought

This exciting new monthly series tackles today's most provocative, fascinating, and relevant issues, giving top opinion makers a forum to explore topics that matter urgently to themselves and their readers. Some will be think pieces. Some will be research oriented. Some will be journalistic in nature. The form is wide open, but the aim is the same: to say things that need saying.

Now available from
THE LIBRARY OF CONTEMPORARY THOUGHT

Coming from
THE LIBRARY OF CONTEMPORARY THOUGHT

*America's most original writers
give you a piece of their minds*

Stephen Jay Gould
Robert Hughes
Jonathan Kellerman
Joe Klein
Walter Mosley
Donna Tartt
Don Imus
Nora Ephron

Look for these titles coming soon from
The Library of Contemporary Thought

STEPHEN JAY GOULD
ROCKS OF AGES
Science and Religion in the Fullness of Life

ROBERT HUGHES
A JERK ON ONE END
Reflections of a Mediocre Fisherman